Muses and Musings: A Poetry Anthology

Table of Contents

In the Still of Night

In the still of night
 The moonlight casts a soft glow,
 Peaceful and serene
 A beacon of hope.
 The moonlight casts a soft glow,
 Guiding us through the darkness
 A beacon of hope
 Guiding us through the night.
 Peaceful and serene
 Guiding us through the darkness
 Guiding us through the night
 A beacon of hope.
 A beacon of hope
 Peaceful and serene
 The moonlight casts a soft glow,
 Guiding us through the darkness.

The River Flows On

The river flows on
    Carving its path through the land
    Nature's timeless song
    An endless journey
    Carving its path through the land
    The water sparkles in the sun
    An endless journey
    Constant and unyielding
    Nature's timeless song
    The water sparkles in the sun
    Constant and unyielding
    An endless journey
    An endless journey
    Nature's timeless song
    Carving its path through the land
    The water sparkles in the sun

The Fire Burns Bright

The fire burns bright,
  As we gather round,
  In the sacred grove,
  We honor the gods,
  With offerings and prayers,
  We celebrate life,
  And all that it holds,
  In this ancient rite,
  We are one with the divine.

The Autumn Leaves Fall

The autumn leaves fall,
   Drifting gently to the ground
   Nature's tapestry
   A symphony of color.
   Drifting gently to the ground
   The autumn breeze whispers,
   A symphony of color
   Dancing in the autumn breeze.
   Nature's tapestry
   The autumn breeze whispers,
   Dancing in the autumn breeze
   A symphony of color.
   A symphony of color
   Nature's tapestry
   Drifting gently to the ground
   The autumn breeze whispers.

The Winds Whisper

The winds whisper,
Through the trees,
As we walk the path,
Of the pagan way,
We honor the elements,
And all that they bring,
We are one with nature,
In this sacred space,
We dance and we sing.

The Moon Rises High

The moon rises high,
    Guiding our way,
    As we dance and sing,
    On this pagan night,
    Beneath the stars,
    We honor the old ways,
    Of our ancestors,
    We are one with the earth,
    And all that it brings.

The Sun Shines Bright

The sun shines bright,
As we awaken,
To the call of the wild,
We honor the earth,
And all its gifts,
We give thanks,
For the abundance and beauty,
Of this pagan life,
We are one with the divine

The Stars Twinkle

The stars twinkle,
In the dark night sky,
As we gather beneath them,
In this sacred space,
We honor the ancestors,
And all that they've given,
We are one with the past,
And all that it holds,
In this pagan life,
We are one with the divine.

Ghosts of Times Forgotten

I am,
    Under the
    Impression
    That all
    Is illusion,
    Just ghosts,
    Of times
    Long forgotten,
    Rising from
    Tartarus
    To haunt
    The present.

Goddess of the Moon

She rises in the sky, a glowing orb,
A symbol of magic, mystery, and power.
She is the keeper of secrets, the ruler of shadows,
The mistress of dreams and desires.
Her light is gentle, yet radiant,
Guiding us through the darkest hours.
She is the queen of the night,
A goddess of the moon, eternal and bright.
We offer her our praise and devotion,
For she is the moon goddess, forever revered.
May she bless us with her grace and favor,
As she reigns supreme in the starry sky.

Left Me All Alone

'Cause, it's a long way from where you are, let me tell you,
    Let me tell you, hey, hey, hey, it's you,
    It's a long way from where you are, let me tell you,
    I am your only girl,
    And all I do is wander,
    Left me all alone
    It's a long way from where I am,
    To where I want to be,
    It's a long way from where I am,
    To where I want to be,
    I can feel you,
    Like a stone you left me
    That you have turned my life around
    There's a light in your eyes,
    It only I can see,
    When it's nighttime and you're looking away
    It's a long way from where I am.

Thanks for the Memories

Thanks for the memories,
    The good and the bad.
    The laughter and the tears,
    The joy and the sadness we've had.
    Thanks for the moments,
    The ones that we shared.
    The times that we laughed,
    And the times that we cared.
    Thanks for the love,
    The kind that's pure and true.
    The love that we gave,
    And the love that we knew.
    Thanks for the memories,
    They'll stay with me forever.
    The ones that we made,
    Together.

Thoughts in My Head

Thoughts swirling in my head,
Words tumbling, unsaid,
I try to capture them all,
In columns, tall and small
I don't know where they come from
Or where they'll go when done
But I write them down, all the same,
In hopes to give them a name
I scribble and I scrawl,
Trying to make sense of it all,
The columns grow and grow,
But I'll never let them go,
For they are a part of me
And I'll keep them, endlessly.

It's Not Your Job

It's not your job, to like me,
    It's mine, to earn your respect,
    It's not your job, to understand me,
    It's mine, to make myself clear, and to connect.
    It's not your job, to accept me,
    It's mine, to be myself, and to be true,
    It's not your job, to approve of me,
    It's mine, to live my life, and to do.
    So, don't worry about liking me,
    Don't worry about understanding me,
    Don't worry about accepting me,
    Just worry about being yourself and being happy.
    For it's not your job, to like me,
    It's mine, to earn your respect,
    It's not your job, to understand me,
    It's mine, to make myself clear, and to connect.
    So, let's just be ourselves, and let it be,
    And let's just focus, on being happy,
    For it's not your job, to like me,
    It's mine, to be myself, and to be true.

My Moment of Zen

Birds singing, leaves rustling,
    The world is alive and bustling,
    I find a quiet place,
    And sit with a smile on my face,
    Inhaling the fragrance of the earth
    I let go of all my mirth,
    In this moment, all is well,
    I am one with the universe, all is swell,
    I close my eyes and take a deep breath,
    Feeling a sense of peace and rest
    This is my moment of Zen,
    Calm and still, I am in
    Complete harmony with all around
    A beautiful, peaceful sound.

Finding Zen

Sitting on a mountaintop
    The world below a distant blur
    I find a moment of peace,
    In the stillness of nature
    Birds chirping, leaves rustling,
    I let go of all my worries,
    Embracing the present moment
    Feeling alive and free
    This is where I find my Zen,
    In the simplicity of the wild.

Coffee in Paris

Sipping coffee in Paris,
A moment of pure bliss.
The city of love and light,
A beautiful sight to miss.
With each warm, rich sip,
My worries begin to slip.
The aroma fills my nose,
And I feel alive, I suppose.
Paris, you have my heart,
In your charming, artful way.
I'll always treasure this moment,
Drinking coffee on this day.

The People Don't Know

The people don't know,
    Where the money goes, where it goes,
    All that you need is love and kindness,
    And that's what you get when you give,
    Where the money goes, where it goes, where this money
    Lives on this way.
    No back door, no blind
    All that you need is love and kindness,
    And that's what you get when you give,
    I've tried, but I can't get it right,
    I've tried giving in, all, all,
    When I'm still waiting on a call
    I can change the day,
    I've come to the right place,
    And I can do it with you,
    When I'm still waiting on a call
    The dream that was so strong
    Can't come true forever,
    'Cause if you leave me.

Memories That Never Rest

Living with PTSD
    Memories that never rest,
    Triggers lurk everywhere,
    But I've learned to do my best,
    To cope and find a way,
    To live with this condition
    I know I'm not alone,
    In this struggle for my own redemption
    So, if you're living with PTSD too,
    Don't give up, there is hope,
    Reach out, seek support,
    You are stronger than you know.

It's Not Even Close at All

When you're gonna leave it all behind you
    I'll be the one who sticks around to show you the way,
    I'll be the one who gets there long before that,
    Well, I got the nerve but I'm afraid to see you go again,
    Oh, it's not the way it used to be,
    We walked together away, and we smiled each other,
    And when you talk it's not even close
    It's not even close at all,
    You know I'll be right there with you,
    I don't want to be who you used to be,
    You've got the nerve to show you how,
    When I leave it all behind you
    I'll be the one who sticks around to show you the way,
    I'll be the one who gets there long before that,
    I know I'll be right there with you.

It's Just a Little Bit

A bit of life
    Baby, give me some,
    Some more
    Just a little bit
    (Baby) Little bit
    (Ain't that a thing of the day, no)
    No use
    (Baby) No, no, no
    It's just a little bit,
    (Ain't that a thing of the day no)
    Don't leave me here to stay for life,
    It's just a little bit,
    (Ain't that a thing of the day, no)
    You're just a bit shy,
    (Ain't that shy, no)
    I know you play,
    (You play) with your toys,
    And I think it's lovely,
    Although there's no music
    I know there's something new,
    Something new to hear,
    Something new to us
    How did I get through.

An Anti-Love Poem

Love is just a myth, a fairy tale we're told,
    A feeling that we chase, but never quite unfold.
    It promises the stars, but gives us nothing in return,
    A cruel deception, that leaves our hearts forever burned.
    The arrows that Cupid shoots, are just arrows of regret,
    A symbol of a broken heart, that we'll never quite forget.
    The roses that we give, are just thorns in disguise,
    A reminder of the pain, that love leaves in our eyes.
    So, let's break the chains of love, and say goodbye to this curse,
    For the love we seek, is just a feeling we'll never nurse.
    No more broken hearts, no more tears we'll have to shed,
    For love is just an illusion, that we'll never truly wed.

I'm Sleep Walking

I'm sleep walking through my days,
Drifting through a foggy haze.
I can't seem to shake this feeling,
That everything is just revealing.
I'm sleep walking through my nights,
Dreaming of distant city lights.
I can't seem to find my way back,
To the land of the fully awake.
I'm sleep walking through my life,
Barely able to survive.
I can't seem to find my place,
In this world that's moving at a rapid pace.
But I know that deep down inside,
There's a spark that's still alive.
And one day I'll wake up and see,
That the world is waiting for me.

There's a Song in the Chaos

Feeling the rhythm from my chaos,
 A dance in the midst of the storm.
 My feet move to the beat of my heart,
 Ignoring the chaos that surrounds.
 There's a song in the chaos of life,
 A melody that echoes within.
 It's the sound of my soul,
 The rhythm of my being.
 I let the music move me,
 As I sway to the beat of my own drum.
 I am in control of my chaos,
 Feeling the rhythm of my soul, come undone.
 The chaos may rage around me,
 But I am at peace within.
 For I have found my rhythm,
 Feeling the beat from my chaos, begin

The Love That Wasn't

Roses are red,
    Violets are blue,
    I thought I found love,
    But it was just a flu.
    My heart was aching,
    My soul was in pain,
    I thought I had found the one,
    But it was just a passing train.
    So now I sit here,
    With my broken heart in hand,
    Wishing I could turn back time,
    To that fateful love stand.

I Can't Help Myself

It feels like a long night,
Like the time you left when you went away
It's too late to call you up,
I know you don't have any friends,
I know it's wrong, but I need them now,
And I can't complain,
Can't complain,
You're looking at a stranger,
With his camera on his hand
You are younger than me,
In a world of broken dreams
I can't help myself,
I'm getting into my own,
You're looking at a stranger,
With his camera on his hand
You are older than me,
In a world of broken dreams
I can't help myself,
I'm getting into my own,
You're looking at a stranger,
With his camera on his hand
You are older than me,
In a world of broken dreams
I can't help myself.

Broken Trust

The pain of betrayal,
It cuts like a knife,
It wounds the soul,
It takes away life.
The trust that's broken,
The promises that are lied upon,
The love that's shattered,
It's a feeling that's hard to don.
The pain of betrayal,
It's a pain that lingers,
It's a pain that hurts,
It's a pain that still fingers.
The hurt and the anger,
The sadness and the despair,
The pain of betrayal,
It's a feeling that's hard to bear.
But I won't let it define me,
I won't let it consume,
I'll rise above it,
I'll find my way through.

Don't Leave Me Now

With my heart
  A little something to make me feel okay,
  I hear the echo of your voice,
  It haunts my nightmares,
  But I'm stronger with every kiss,
  So, don't leave me now,
  Don't leave me now,
  Don't leave me now,
  I want to be your friend,
  I'll be your friend,
  I'll be your friend,
  The time has come but you don't want me in your life,
  You couldn't give me the time,
  No matter how I try or how far I'll run,
  You don't have the heart to make me breathe,
  So, I'm thinking maybe tonight,
  I'll give the part of me that you have never shown,
  So please don't leave me now,
  Don't leave me now,
  Don't leave me now,
  I'm not the one you want to miss.

Human Nature

The monstrosity of human nature,
It's a darkness that dwells within,
It's a monster that lurks,
It's a monster that's always been.
The cruelty and the violence,
The greed and the hate,
The selfishness and the ignorance,
They all seal our fate.
The monstrosity of human nature,
It's a cancer that eats us alive,
It's a poison that destroys us,
It's a poison we can't survive.
But we must not give in,
We must not succumb,
We must fight this monster,
We must overcome.
The monstrosity of human nature,
It's a battle that we must win,
We must rise above it,
We must let the light shine within.

Joy and Abandon

She danced in the rain,
With joy and abandon.
Her heart was alive,
As she twirled and spun.
The raindrops kissed her skin,
As she moved to the beat.
She let go of all her fears,
And moved two feet.
The rain was her stage,
And she was the star.
In that moment, she was free,
Dancing from afar.
The rain may come and go,
But her spirit will remain.
She danced in the rain,
And it was all worth the pain.

Of Anything

You can't get enough and don't know,
    You can't get enough.
    And then in spiraling out
    You know you can't get enough.
    Just look at me,
    I've been waiting.
    Never stop.
    Every word
    I can't live.
    I just can't give up.
    And now I'll never get much.
    Of anything,
    Never be fine.
    And then in spiraling out
    You know you can't get enough.
    Just look at me,
    I've been waiting.
    Never stop.
    Every word
    I can't live.
    I just can't give up.
    And now I'll never get much.
    Of anything,
    I just can't give up.
    I just can't give up.

Unrequited Self-love

Self-love seems, so often, unrequited,
    It's a love, that's so often, ignored,
    It's a love, that's so often, neglected,
    It's a love, that's so often, deplored.
    Self-love seems, so often, unrequited,
    It's a love, that's so often, misunderstood,
    It's a love, that's so often, underestimated,
    It's a love, that's so often, misconstrued.
    Self-love seems, so often, unrequited,
    It's a love, that's so often, unappreciated
    It's a love, that's so often, undervalued,
    It's a love, that's so often, denigrated.
    So, don't neglect, your own self-love,
    Don't neglect, your own self-worth,
    Don't neglect, your own self-esteem,
    Don't neglect, your own self-birth.
    For self-love seems, so often, unrequited,
    It's a love, that's so often, ignored,
    It's a love, that's so often, neglected,
    It's a love, that's so often, deplored.

Oh No

When it's too hard to sleep,
    The moment my eyes start staring off in the moonlight,
    I'll sit and you can come to me,
    And everything's going to be alright,
    If you wait for me to go quietly,
    I'll wait for sleep,
    You can wait until I'm going home again,
    Oh no
    You need a thing to keep,
    And I belong to your
    Hospital room
    I'm waiting at the computer,
    When I wake up every night
    Just wondering where I'll be,
    When I get home
    It all becomes crystal,
    It all becomes a crystal ball,
    Every time you look at me,
    You'll be a million miles away,
    I'll take care of everything,
    Just give me just as much as I can give,
    Everything as I can give.

On Angel's Wings

On angel's wings, I take flight,
A journey so pure, that's always bright.
It's a journey of magic, and of wonders so great,
On angel's wings, a journey that's late.
It's a journey of beauty, and of love so true,
On angel's wings, a journey that's new.
It's a journey of hope, and of dreams so wild,
On angel's wings, a journey that's mild.
It's a journey of peace, and of serenity so deep,
On angel's wings, a journey that's steep.
It's a journey of magic, and of wonders so great,
On angel's wings, a journey that's late.
So, I take flight, with a heart that's true,
On angel's wings, a journey that's new.
A journey of magic, for you and me,
On angel's wings, a journey of enlightenment, you'll see.

Why Do You Love Me

I can't stop loving you.
    You know I can't stop, can't stop love again.
    I am not a stranger; I don't hail from here.
    I hail from somewhere, hail from somewhere.
    I've been born here before you.
    I was born in England, but I never knew where to turn.
    Where are you now, more perfect now?
    Why do you love me?
    I know you've been hiding away.
    Where are you now, more perfect now?
    Where are you now, more perfect now?
    Why do you love me?
    I know you've been hiding away.
    Where are you now, more perfect now?
    Where are you now, more perfect now?
    Why do you love me?
    I know you've been hiding away.
    Where are you now, more perfect now.

Bless the mothers

Bless the mothers,
    The ones who love and nurture.
    The ones who care and protect,
    Through any kind of weather.
    Bless the mothers,
    The ones who give their all.
    The ones who sacrifice and put others first,
    Despite the toll it takes on their own soul.
    Bless the mothers,
    The ones who never give up.
    The ones who fight and stand their ground,
    For the ones they hold dear and love.
    Bless the mothers,
    The ones who make the world go round.
    For without them, we'd be lost,
    But with them, we are found.

It's Time to Start, Baby

It's time to start, baby.
   I know that you're hurting, baby.
   Now it's my turn to doze, baby.
   Wipe away the tears, baby!
   Save me, save me!
   It's time to start, baby.
   I know that you're hurting, baby.
   It's time to start, baby.
   I know that you're hurting, baby.
   So I am, I'm here to say this.
   I'm here to say this, baby.
   I'm better off dead.
   Better off dead, better off dead
   Better off dead, better off dead come what may.
   Because I'm better off dead.
   Better off dead, better off dead
   Better off dead come what may.
   Because I'm better off dead.
   Better off dead, better off dead
   Better off dead come what may.

Mirror, Mirror

Mirror, mirror on the wall
    Who is the fairest of them all?
    I stare at my reflection,
    Trying to find perfection,
    But the more I look, the more I see,
    The beauty within, shining bright and free,
    I am more than a selfie, a filter, or a pose,
    I am a unique individual, with my own path to choose,
    I embrace my flaws and imperfections,
    For they make me who I am, no need for corrections,
    I am enough, just as I am,
    And that, dear mirror, is my enlightenment plan.

The Loss of a Loved One

The loss of a loved one,
    It's a pain that never fades,
    It's a grief that lingers,
    It's a void that can't be filled.
    The memories that we shared,
    They bring both joy and sorrow,
    The love that we had,
    It's a love that I'll borrow.
    The loss of a loved one,
    It's a loss that I can't comprehend,
    It's a loss that I feel,
    It's a loss that I must contend.
    The emptiness that I feel,
    It's a feeling that I can't describe,
    The loss of a loved one,
    It's a feeling that I can't hide.
    But I'll hold on to the love,
    The love that we shared,
    I'll hold on to the memories,
    And they'll keep me repaired.

Under the Full Moon's Glow

Under the full moon's glow
Glow, my heart beats fast.
I see my love come near,
Near, with quick and light step past.
Past, the doubts that made me shake,
Shake, with joy and elation.
My heart beats fast to see,
See, my love approach my station.
Station, where I've waited long,
Long, with patience and faith.
Now, at last, she's here,
Here, with me, by my side, forever stay.
Forever, together, my love and I,
I, who will love her more.
Under the full moon's glow,
Glow, our love will shine and soar.

That There's an Answer
I will take you by the hand,
And I will show you the way to find you,
I can tell you 'bout out loud,
So, don't keep me waiting on that,
Can I get you my love again,
Would you make up for what you had done to me,
What you made me afraid about
I don't want to hear you say,
That I'm not so scared of being alone
'Cause I know there's an answer,
And it'll only come as no surprise,
What I would want is for you to know,
That there's an answer
And it'll only come as no surprise,
What I would want you to know
Don't take all the pain,
I don't want to see you cry, cry, cry, cry,
Like the tears come to me.

Tortured Soul

My tortured soul is filled with sorrow,
My spirit weighed down by the pain.
The darkness looms around me like a sparrow,
Twisting my heart and stirring my bane.
The night sky casts a dismal hue,
My eyes are tired from the wear.
My soul is trapped in an inky view,
Awaiting a break from the fear.
The stars twinkle in the night,
The moon glows with a pale light.
But still my heart is filled with fright,
For I am lost in a sea of night.
My anguish is deep and unseen,
My tears they fall like rain.
My cries unheard, my soul unclean,
I'm lost in darkness and pain.

I am the Bulletproof Poet

I am the bulletproof poet,
    Unbreakable and unshakable,
    My words are my armor,
    My pen is my sword.
    I march forward,
    Through the fray and the chaos,
    Unafraid and undaunted,
    For my poetry is my shield.
    I am the bulletproof poet,
    Invincible and indomitable,
    My rhymes are my fortress,
    My verse is my strength.
    I stand tall,
    Amidst the gunfire and the insults,
    Unwavering and unyielding,
    For my poetry is my salvation.
    I am the bulletproof poet,
    Unstoppable and unvanquished,
    My poetry is my power,
    My words are my courage.

Nightmares Pretending to be Daydreams
    They come to me in the night,
    These nightmares pretending to be daydreams.
    They wrap me in a cloak of fear,
    And fill my head with screams.
    They twist and turn and warp,
    Until I don't know what is real.

They play with my emotions,
And make me feel like I'm not able to heal.
But I know that they're not real,
These nightmares pretending to be daydreams.
They're just shadows in my mind,
Hauntings of things I've seen.
So, I close my eyes and take a deep breath,
And remind myself that they're not true.
And when I wake up in the morning,
I know that I can make it through.

We're Still Making Progress
We're still making progress,
Like we promised then, then we promised then,
There's not a day I don't wake up with the blues on
And all the reasons why I said I never would,
But I'll miss you when all the good time just disappears,
'Cause I've still got the blues on
And I'm not feeling the good times I know,
Will be there when they fade away,
'Cause I've still got the blues on
The days and nights we had, we did,
But time has turned cold, has no longer made love,
But we've still got the blues on
And I'm just dreaming of a love in my life,
That lasts forever, that lasts forever,
And I still have the blues on
And I'm not feeling the good times I know.

Eternal Truths

Bornless, thou art beyond the reach of time,
Thy essence, pure and free from earthly woe.
In thy eternal realm, all is divine,
And mortals bow in reverence down below.
The stars themselves do homage to thy name,
In thy transcendent presence, they do shine.
And every soul that yearns for truth and fame,
Finds solace in thy grace that's always thine.
Oh Bornless, thou art the source of all,
Of light and life, of love and liberty.
In thee alone, we find our final call,
And seek to dwell in thy infinity.
So let us raise our voices in thy praise,
And bask in thy immortal, radiant rays.

The Blade of Endurance

The pain you feel today is the strength you feel tomorrow,
A fire that burns within and turns your sorrow into power.
It takes the broken pieces and forges them into a shield,
A symbol of resilience, that stands tall and never yields.
The hurt you carry now, will make you stronger in the end,
A weapon in the battle, to conquer all that you may bend.
The scars that line your soul, are stories that you can share,
Proof of how you rose above, and how much you truly care.
So don't let the pain defeat you, hold your head up high,
Remember what you're fighting for and let your spirit fly.
For every step you take, is a step closer to the prize,
And the pain you feel today, will be the strength you feel tomorrow.

You Call

Do you want to do me right?
Tell me how to be the boy I wanna be,
What you need is something real,
Something real so much bigger than life
And you want to do me right,
And you want to do me right,
Well, you called,
I cut you down to size in your last night,
I said I'd put your soul to sleep,
and now
you call,
I scream,
I know it ain't me,
who made you wild,
and I know that all you ever wanted,
Was the chance to use my voice,
I know 'cause you spoke so damn strong,
Now I know,
Because I fought to the end
And I bleed to your side,
You call,
I want to do you right,
I know,
I've tried,
To heal your wounded.
Simplicity
Simplicity is the ultimate sophistication,
It's the art, of stripping away, the excess,
It's the beauty, of finding the essence, and the core,
It's the elegance, of letting go, of the more.

Simplicity is the ultimate sophistication,
It's the clarity, of seeing things, for what they are,
It's the peace, of letting go, of the distractions,
It's the calm, of finding focus, and the sparks.
Simplicity is the ultimate sophistication,
It's the grace, of being true, to oneself,
It's the honesty, of being authentic, and real,
It's the humility, of letting go, of the wealth.

It's Written in The Stars
To see it through
No place, no distance
To go and never listen
The night could only waste time
So, take me away,
Show me how I must go,
It's written in the stars,
And how they sing a song for me,
But if, dear, world will end soon,
If the people can't be satisfied
Tell me who must supply the fuel.
God is a great, great, great creator.
Tell me who is to die,
Tell me now a world is dying out,
Show me how I must go,
But once upon a time a time of need
So, tell me who, dear, world will end soon.
It's written in the stars,
And how they sing a song for me,
But if, dear, world will end soon,
If the people can't be satisfied.

The Truth

The truth is written in the fabric of the universe,
    In the patterns and the stars.
    It's etched in the very DNA of life,
    And in the beating of our hearts.
    It's hidden in the mysteries of time,
    In the mysteries of space.
    It's revealed in the whispers of the wind,
    And in the look on a loved one's face.
    We may not always see it clearly,
    It may be shrouded in doubt.
    But the truth is always there,
    Waiting to be found.
    So, let's seek the truth with open hearts,
    And let it guide us on our way.
    For when we align with the truth,
    We can find peace and grace each day.
    So, let's embrace simplicity, and find peace,
    Let's let go, of the distractions, and the noise,
    Let's find focus, and clarity, and grace,
    And let's be true, to ourselves, and our joys.
    For simplicity, is the ultimate sophistication,
    It's the key, to finding happiness, and serenity.

Loki and the Nine Realms

Loki and the nine realms, a story so old,
    A tale of mischief, that's never been told.
    It's a story of magic, and of powers so great,
    Loki and the nine realms, a story that's late.
    It's a story of trickery, and of cunning so sly,
    Loki and the nine realms, a story that's high.
    It's a story of deception, and of secrets untold,
    Loki and the nine realms, a story that's bold.
    It's a story of adventure, and of danger so real,
    Loki and the nine realms, a story that's keen.
    It's a story of magic, and of powers so great,
    Loki and the nine realms, a story that's fate.
    So, I listen to it, with a heart that's true,
    Loki and the nine realms, a story that's new.
    A tale of mischief, that's for the bold
    Loki and the nine realms, a story that will forever be told.

The Path to Inner Peace

The path to inner peace
Is paved with pictures,
Of our true selves, unedited
The more we capture,
The more we see,
Beyond the masks we wear
And all that society
Expects us to be,
Until we find our way
To the core of who we are
In every selfie, a reminder
To embrace our true selves,
No matter what they are.

Naming the Goddess

Naming the goddess, a rite so old,
    A tradition that's sacred, that's never been told.
    It's a rite of honor, and of respect so great,
    Naming the goddess, a tradition that's late.
    It's a rite of devotion, and of love so pure,
    Naming the goddess, a tradition that's sure.
    It's a rite of worship, and of secrets untold,
    Naming the goddess, a tradition that's bold.
    It's a rite of reverence, and of honor so true,
    Naming the goddess, a tradition that's new.
    It's a rite of devotion, and of respect so great,
    Naming the goddess, a tradition that's fate.
    So, I stand before it, with a heart that's true,
    Naming the goddess, a tradition that's new.
    A rite of honor, that's for sure,
    Naming the goddess, a tradition for the pure.

I Believed I Could

I believed I could, but I overslept,
    So, I didn't, get up and make a start,
    I let the comfort, of my bed, hold me back,
    And I let my dreams, keep me apart.
I believed I could, but I overslept,
And I let the day, slip away,
I let the moments, pass me by
And I let my goals, fade away.
But I won't give up, and I won't despair,
I won't let one setback, hold me down,
I'll get up, and I'll try again,
And I'll turn this day, around.
For I believe in myself, and my potential,
I believe in my dreams, and my goals,
I believe that I can do it,
I believe that I can make it whole.
So, I'll get up, and I'll start anew,
I'll seize the day, and make it mine
I'll believe in myself, and I'll do it,
I'll overcome, and I'll shine.

Proud to be a Navy Veteran

I'm proud to be a Navy veteran,
    To have served my country with all my might.
    To have stood tall and strong,
    Through the darkest of nights.
    I've sailed the seven seas,
    And braved the raging storms.
    I've stood my ground,
    And faced countless foes.
    I've seen the world,
    And all its wonders and woes.
    And through it all,
    I've never lost my hope.
    So, I stand tall,
    With my head held high.
    Proud to be a Navy veteran,
    And to the stars I'll reach for the sky.

Look Within

Look within, and search, for who you were, before the world, told you,
who to be
    That's the way, it is, and that's the way, it'll be,
    With a quest, that's deep, and meaningful, and authentic
    With a meaning, that's authentic, and deep, and meaningful
    Look within, and search, for who you were, before the world, told
you, who to be
    That's the way, it feels, and that's the way, it looks,
    With a feeling, that's true, and genuine, and real
    With a reality, that's real, and genuine, and true
    Look within, and search, for who you were, before the world, told
you, who to be
    That's the way, it sounds, and that's the way, it tastes,
    With a sound, that's authentic, and sincere, and honest
    With a taste, that's honest, and sincere, and authentic
    So, don't be afraid, to look within, or to search, or to discover,
    Don't be afraid, to be yourself, or to be genuine, or to be authentic,
    Don't be afraid, to be true, or to be real, or to be sincere,
    Don't be afraid, to be honest, or to be open, or to be vulnerable.
    For look within, and search, for who you were, before the world,
told you, who to be
    That's the way, it is, and that's the way, it'll be,
    With a quest, that's deep, and meaningful, and authentic
    With a meaning, that's authentic, and deep, and meaningful.

If You Don't Know the Devil

If you don't know the devil,
Then you don't know me.
For I have danced with him,
In the depths of misery.
He has shown me the dark,
The shadows of my soul.
He has led me astray,
And taken his toll.
But I have learned from him,
In ways that I can't explain.
He has shaped me, molded me,
And left his mark on my veins.
So, if you don't know the devil,
Then you don't know me.
For he is a part of me,
And I am a part of him.

The Wheel of the Year

The Wheel of the year spins on,
    Through the seasons, one by one.
    From the dark of winter's cold embrace,
    To the light and warmth of summer's face.
    Imbalance and balance, dark and light,
    The wheel turns through the day and night.
    Solstice and equinox, quarter days,
    Mark the passing of the seasons in their own way.
    Samhain, Yule, Imbolc, and Ostara,
    Beltane, Litha, Lammas, and Mabon.
    Each a sacred holiday of its own,
    Celebrated by Wiccans all alone.
    The wheel of the year, a sacred cycle,
    Connects us to the earth and to the divine.
    We honor the seasons, and all that they bring,
    As we dance and sing and honor the divine king.

House of Five Dragons

House of five dragons, a home so grand,
    A place of magic, that's always manned.
    It's a home of power, and of secrets untold,
    House of five dragons, a place that's old.
    It's a home of wisdom, and of knowledge so true,
    House of five dragons, a place that's new.
    It's a home of magic, and of powers so great,
    House of five dragons, a place that's late.
    It's a home of mystery, and of secrets so deep,
    House of five dragons, a place that's steep.
    It's a home of magic, and of wonders untold,
    House of five dragons, a place that's old.
    So, I stand before it, with a heart that's true,
    House of five dragons, a place that's new
    A home of magic, and majesty
    House of five dragons, wonderful and free.

I Just Wanna Be Touched

I get myself caught in the middle,
Where the stars don't shine for the stars in my eyes.
I am just a stranger in this town, a stranger in town.
I've been around but never quite reached the level I needed till today.
I don't wanna be somebody's boyfriend.
I won't give you anything, not what you need.
I just wanna be yourself.
I just wanna be touched.
Wish I would have told you so,
So many things I never need said.
They are all in my heart,
But there's just one thing I can't tell you.
I don't wanna be somebody's boyfriend.
I won't give you anything, not what you need.
I just wanna be myself.
I just wanna be touched.

Life's Uncertain

Life's uncertain, so eat dessert first,
    Indulge, in the sweetness, and the joy,
    Life's uncertain, so savor each bite,
    Life's uncertain, so don't be coy.
    Life's uncertain, so enjoy the moment,
    Life's uncertain, so make it count,
    Life's uncertain, so don't wait,
    Life's uncertain, so don't discount.
    Life's uncertain, so don't hold back,
    Life's uncertain, so let yourself go,
    Life's uncertain, so live each day, to the fullest,
    Life's uncertain, so let your spirit, flow.
    So, don't wait, to have dessert.
    Don't wait, to live your life,
    Don't wait, to embrace the moment,
    Don't wait, to cause some strife.
    For life's uncertain, so eat dessert first,
    Life's uncertain, so enjoy the sweet
    Life's uncertain, so make the most, of each day,
    Life's uncertain, so don't miss a beat.

The Fanatics

You're my greatest fan,
    And my only fan
    This is for the fans, the fans,
    And the fanatics
    To whom you most owe
    This is for the fans, the fans,
    And the fans
    Who are so dear to you,
    They're the greatest fans,
    There's something about this story,
    That really means a lot,
    It seems so simple,
    How you slipped into my heart
    This love was passed on the way,
    And now our goodbyes
    Drive me crazy,
    It's the hardest thing to do,
    'Cause you slipped right in
    And I'm so thankful,
    But there's no more pretending,
    There's no more about this guy,
    'Cause he's slipping 'neath my wings,
    I can't stop myself from remembering,
    A miracle is comin' to stay.

Death and Magic

The darkness looms ever larger in my life
A constant threat, forever in sight
I search the shadows for something bright,
But the light I find is never quite right,
The dead linger around in my thoughts,
Their presence constantly in my mind
I cannot escape the magic I've sought,
Death and magic intertwined.
My life was once full of cheer,
But now I'm held in the grip of fear,
The shadows that haunt me never clear
My heart can no longer hold back the tears.
The darkness has taken away the light,
Death has infected me with its blight,
My life is now forever night,
The darkness is my only delight.
My life is consumed by death and magic,
A battle I can never win,
The tide of despair is always dramatic,
As I find myself ever deeper in.

Showgirls and Aliens

Showgirls and aliens, a scene so strange,
A world of glamour, that's always deranged.
It's a world of magic, and of wonders so great,
Showgirls and aliens, a scene that's late.
It's a world of mystery, and of secrets untold,
Showgirls and aliens, a scene that's old.
It's a world of glamour, and of beauty so pure,
Showgirls and aliens, a scene that's sure.
It's a world of glitter, and of lights so bright,
Showgirls and aliens, a scene that's light.
It's a world of magic, and of wonders so great,
Showgirls and aliens, a scene that's late.
So, I stand, and I watch, with a heart that's true,
Showgirls and aliens, a scene that's new.
A world of glamour, full of joy and delight,
Showgirls and aliens, a scene that feels just right.

A journey Awaits Us

A journey awaits us, a path of fate,
The winding road that we must take,
A blaze of glory, a challenge we face,
To discover our own destiny in this place.
We must bravely carry on, through joy and strife,
Learning from the moments of our life,
And never forget the beauty we find,
In the wonders of this world that we bind.
Though treacherous the journey may be,
We must never forget who we want to be,
And strive to reach a better place,
Where we can be our best and embrace.

Lies Don't Care

Lies don't care about the truth,
    They don't care about the pain.
    They don't care about the consequences,
    They just keep spinning and spinning again.
    They twist and turn and manipulate,
    They try to confuse and deceive.
    They'll say whatever it takes,
    To get what they want, they'll never leave.
    But the truth, it always comes out,
    It's a force that can't be denied.
    It may take some time to surface,
    But it will always be a guide.
    So don't be fooled by the lies,
    Don't let them cloud your sight.
    Seek the truth and hold on tight,
    For it is the only thing that's right.

I'm a Force of Nature

I am just sunshine, mixed with a little hurricane,
I am a force, of nature, and of will,
I am a storm, of emotion, and of fire,
I am a tempest, that rages, and that thrill.
I am just sunshine, mixed with a little hurricane,
I am a force, of determination, and of drive,
I am a gust, of passion, and of desire,
I am a whirlwind, that strives, and that thrive.
I am just sunshine, mixed with a little hurricane,
I am a force, of change, and of growth,
I am a breeze, of transformation, and of evolution,
I am a gale, that moves, and that both.
So, don't underestimate me, or my power,
Don't underestimate me, or my might,
Don't underestimate me, or my spirit,
Don't underestimate me, or my light.
For I am just sunshine, mixed with a little hurricane,
I am a force, of nature, and of will,
I am a storm, of emotion, and of fire,
I am a tempest, that rages, and that thrill.

Small Steps

Taking small steps, in being myself, every day
    That's the way, I find my way,
      With a journey, that's gradual, and steady
      With a path, that's gradual, and ready
      Taking small steps, in being myself, every day
      That's the way, I discover my true self,
      With a process, that's ongoing, and evolving
      With a growth, that's ongoing, and dissolving
      Taking small steps, in being myself, every day
      That's the way, I embrace my uniqueness,
      With a courage, that's growing, and unafraid
      With a strength, that's growing, and unafraid
      So, don't rush, the process, of self-discovery,
      Don't rush, the journey, of self-exploration,
      Don't rush, the path, of self-acceptance,
      Don't rush, the growth, of self-expression.
      For taking small steps, in being myself, every day
      That's the way, I find my way,
      With a journey, that's gradual, and steady
      With a path, that's gradual, and ready.

The Burn of Desire

The heat between you and me is burning us up,
    A flame that never fades, a fire that won't stop.
    Our passion consumes us, we can't get enough,
    The temperature rises, it's too hot to touch.
    We ignite each other, with a spark so bright,
    A blaze that illuminates the darkest night.
    Our love is a conflagration, we can't deny,
    The heat between you and me, it never dies.
    We're like two infernos, melting into one,
    A wildfire that spreads, a never-ending fun.
    Our hearts beat together, our souls are intertwined,
    The heat between you and me is burning us up, all the time.

What Am I To Do

In the morning
>I think about where we'll be,
>I can see you again.
>You're a devil to the heart.
>What am I to do?
>What am I to do?
>Tell you I'm sorry, baby!
>I'm sorry, no way it's going to happen,
>Gets me out, though I know it's a lie,
>Telling you I'm sorry, but it's a sad story,
>Can't pretend you're not gonna feel the way I do,
>I'm really over you.
>What am I to do?
>What am I to do?
>Tell you I'm sorry, baby!
>I'm sorry, no way it's going to happen.
>Gets me out, though I know it's a lie.
>Telling you baby I'm sorry, but it's a sad story.

Death's Embrace

The chill of death's embrace,
It's a cold, icy touch,
It sends shivers down my spine,
It's a feeling I don't like much.
The end that it brings,
It's a finality,
It's a closing of the curtain,
On this life's reality.
The fear that it brings,
It's a natural response,
But I'll face it with courage,
And try to be nonchalant.
The chill of death's embrace,
It's a journey we must all take,
But I'll hold my head high,
And for death, I won't quake.

Don't Judge Me

I'm not too lazy, just a master, of energy conservation,

I'm not a sloth, or a slacker, or a loafer,

I'm not a procrastinator, or a dawdler, or a lagger,

I'm just a wise, and a savvy, and a frugal adopter.

I'm not too lazy, just a master, of energy conservation,

I'm not a quitter, or a coward, or a failure,

I'm not a defeatist, or a pessimist, or a grouch,

I'm just a wise, and a savvy, and a frugal tailor.

I'm not too lazy, just a master, of energy conservation,

I'm not a waste, or a burden, or a drain,

I'm not a liability, or a nuisance, or a pain,

I'm just a wise, and a savvy, and a frugal refrain.

So, don't judge me, or my style,

Don't judge me, or my pace,

Don't judge me, or my approach,

Don't judge me, or my race,

For I'm not too lazy, just a master, of energy conservation,

I'm not a sloth, or a slacker, or a loafer,

I'm just a wise, and a savvy, and a frugal adopter,

I'm just a wise, and a savvy, and a frugal tailor.

Forget What You Know

Forget what you know and remember how you feel,
    Leave the facts and figures behind,
    Step away from the books and screens,
    And let your senses come to life.
    Remember the way the wind felt on your skin,
    The sound of the birds singing in the trees,
    The way the sun warmed your face,
    And the way the rain fell on your cheeks.
    Forget what you know and remember how you feel,
    The way love made your heart race,
    The way a child's laughter filled you with joy,
    And the way a friend's touch brought comfort and grace.
    Forget the information that clutters your mind,
    And remember the emotions that touch your soul,
    For in the feelings, we hold dear,
    We find the truest, most beautiful goal.

I Don't Wanna Go Home

I don't wanna go home.
I don't wanna go home.
It sure feels nice.
A girl that I know.
And she's a hell of a woman.
I can't believe it's been almost that long.
Since she turned the lights down
I can't believe it's been too long.
Since she turned the lights down
I can't believe it's been too long since.
Since she turned the lights down
I can't believe it's been too long.
Since she turned the lights down
We are on the ground.
I'm on the ground.
I got my head around it all.
The last thing I wanted was you by my side.
Any more than the party's over
I don't wanna go home.
I don't wanna go home.
It sure feels nice.

No Danger Baby

We'll all leave on our own free choice,
It makes you come running home alone,
Why don't you take little boy high up in your hand,
It's not your fault he's so quiet,
Why don't you take little boy high up in his hand,
No danger baby,
Ain't no need to talk,
If you feel you're lonely
When you want to argue
Let the decision come to you,
If you feel you're lonely
When you need to run away
Let the moment come when you need to run home,
Why don't you take little boy high up in your hand,
No danger baby,
Ain't no need to walk,
Don't wanna hear that little boy scream,
Oh no, no, no
'Cause you make the call.

I Have Found Myself

I have lost myself,
    Every day
    I have lost myself.
    Every chance that I've taken,
    Every hour that I've missed somebody's kiss.
    Every mile
    I have lost myself.
    I have been found.
    I have found myself.
    I have found myself.
    I am caught between the answers that I've found.
    It's a perfect storm.
    A foolish pace the sky is falling down,
    But I try to find the answers,
    find the answers!
    I find the answers, I find the answers.
    You called my bluff.
    So, find the answers you've found,
find the answers, you found the answers, you found the answers
you found!
    Find the answers you've found!

Friendlier

Trust me! I'm friendlier, than you think,
    I'm not as tough, or as rough, as I seem,
    I'm not as guarded, or as closed off, as I appear,
    I'm not as distant, or as aloof, as I seem.
    Trust me! I'm friendlier, than you think,
    I'm not as cold, or as unfeeling, as I act,
    I'm not as tough, or as hard, as I show,
    I'm not as distant, or as apart, as I act.
    Trust me! I'm friendlier, than you think,
    I'm just a little shy, or a little hesitant,
    I'm just a little reserved, or a little cautious,
    I'm just a little nervous, or a little self-conscious.
    So, don't be afraid, to approach me.
    Don't be afraid, to say hi,
    Don't be afraid, to be friendly,
    Don't be afraid, to give it a try.
    For I am friendlier, than you think,
    I'm just a little shy, or a little hesitant,
    But I'm open, and I'm warm,
    And I'm willing, to be friends, with you.

Instruction Manual

I come with an instruction manual,
    Handle with care
    I'm not like other people, or things,
    I'm not easy, or simple, or bare.
    I come with an instruction manual,
    Handle with care
    I'm complex, and intricate, and deep,
    I'm layered, and rich, and steep.
    I come with an instruction manual,
    Handle with care
    I'm fragile, and sensitive, and delicate,
    I'm vulnerable, and emotional, and upsettable.
    So, take your time, and read the manual,
    Take your time, and follow the guide,
    Take your time, and be patient,
    Take your time and be kind.
    For I come with an instruction manual
    Handle with care
    I'm not like other people, or things,
    I'm not easy, or simple, or bare.

Punk Rock Princess

She's a punk rock princess,
    With a heart of gold.
    She's got a fire in her soul,
    That can never be controlled.
    She doesn't follow the rules,
    She makes her own way.
    She marches to the beat of her own drum,
    And she won't be swayed.
    She's got a razor-sharp tongue,
    And a fierce sense of pride.
    She won't let anyone bring her down,
    Or fill her with false pride.
    She's a force to be reckoned with,
    This punk rock princess divine.
    She's got the power to change the world,
    And she's not afraid to shine.

Why Walk When You Can Dance?

Why walk when you can dance?
    Why trudge through life, with heavy feet
    When you can let go, and move to the beat,
    Why waste your time, with mundane steps
    When you can let your body, be free and expressive.
    Why walk when you can dance?
    Why miss out on the joy, and the thrill,
    Of moving to the music, with abandon and will
    Why settle for mediocrity, when you can soar,
    On the wings of rhythm, and the beat of your heart.
    So, don't be afraid, to let your body loose,
    Don't hold back, or let fear hold sway,
    Just let go, and let the music move you,
    And dance, with all your heart, and soul.
    For life is too short, to hold back and hide,
    It's meant to be lived, with passion and pride,
    So why walk, when you can dance?
    Embrace the music, and let your spirit enhance!

All The Heartache Through the Day

All the pain I feel all day.
    All the heartache through the day
    All the tears the tears I'm cryin' for all the time I spend.
    When I'm around, it's such a waste of time.
    I'm in a town, you're everywhere.
    A new love has turned for the cold.
    No one has known better for love.
    A different time, a new love
    Now it feels just the same.
    The lights are always the same.
    I'm in a town, you're everywhere.
    A new love has turned for the cold.
    No one has known better for love.
    A different time, a new love
    All the hours are the same.
    I'm in a place, you're everywhere.
    A new love has turned for the cold.
    No one has known better for love.

Free Trip Around the Sun

Life on earth is expensive,
But it includes a free trip, around the sun,
It's a journey, that we all must take,
A journey, that's filled with ups and downs, and fun.
Life on earth is expensive,
But it includes a free trip, through time,
It's a journey, that we all must make,
A journey, that's filled with joy, and with grime.
Life on earth is expensive,
But it includes a free trip, through the unknown
It's a journey, that we all must brave,
A journey, that's filled with twists and turns, and with stone.
So, let's embrace the journey, and the cost,
Let's embrace the ups, and the downs,
Let's embrace the twists, and the turns,
Let's embrace the unknown, and the profound.
For life on earth is expensive
But it includes a free trip, around the sun,
It's a journey, that we all must take,
A journey, that's filled with ups and downs, and fun.

Black Coffee and Big Cigars

Black coffee and big cigars,
    A taste of the dark and mysterious.
    A sip of the bitter, a puff of the smoke,
    A moment of peace in a world full of choke.
    The aroma wafts through the air,
    A reminder of a simpler time and place.
    A sip and a puff, and the troubles all fade,
    As the mind drifts away to a better space.
    Black coffee and big cigars,
    A symbol of a rugged, independent soul.
    A sign of a man who's not afraid to be himself,
    And who knows that life is but a fleeting goal.
    So, raise your cup and light your stogie,
    And take a moment to just be.
    For in this simple pleasure we find,
    A small bit of eternity.

Blossoms in Japan

The blossoms in Japan,
    They are a sight to behold.
    Their petals soft and delicate,
    Their colors pink and gold.
    They bloom for just a moment,
    A fleeting, fragile thing.
    But in that brief, beautiful moment,
    They bring joy and peace to everything.
    The cherry blossoms are a symbol,
    Of the impermanence of life.
    They remind us to embrace each day,
    And not to cause strife.
    So, when the blossoms come to bloom,
    Take a moment to stop and stare.
    And let their beauty fill your heart,
    With love and joy beyond compare.

I Am Who I Am

I am who I am, your approval isn't needed,
    I don't need, your validation, or your seal,
    I don't need, your permission, or your nod,
    I don't need, your acceptance, or your appeal.
    I am who I am, your approval isn't needed,
    I am my own person, and my own being,
    I am my own identity, and my own self,
    I am my own story, and my own meaning.
    I am who I am, your approval isn't needed,
    I am unique, and I am special,
    I am different, and I am one of a kind,
    I am extraordinary, and I am essential.
    So, don't try, to change me,
    Don't try, to mold me,
    Don't try, to define me,
    Don't try, to control me,
    For I am who I am, your approval isn't needed,
    I am my own person, and my own being,
    I am my own identity, and my own self,
    I am my own story, and my own meaning.

Tales of Madness and Mayhem

Tales of madness and mayhem, stories so wild,
A journey of chaos, that's always compiled.
It's a journey of madness, and of trouble so great,
Tales of madness and mayhem, a journey that's late.
It's a journey of mischief, and of chaos so sly,
Tales of madness and mayhem, a journey that's high.
It's a journey of destruction, and of secrets untold,
Tales of madness and mayhem, a journey that's old.
It's a journey of danger, and of terror so real,
Tales of madness and mayhem, a journey that's keen.
It's a journey of madness, and of trouble so great,
Tales of madness and mayhem, a journey that's fate.
So, I listen to it, with a heart that's true,
Tales of madness and mayhem, a journey that's new.
A journey of chaos, made for Eris,
Tales of madness and mayhem, a journey that's chaotic bliss.

The Great Equalizer

Death, the great equalizer
    No one escapes its cold grip,
    It comes for rich and poor alike,
    No matter how we try to slip.
    It takes our loved ones in its embrace,
    Leaves us bereft and alone,
    But death is just a part of life,
    It's a journey we must undertake alone.
    So, let us cherish every moment,
    And hold our loved ones close,
    For death will come for us one day
    But until then, let's make the most.
    Of every breath and every day
    And live our lives with purpose and grace,
    For death will come, but it can't steal,
    The love and memories we embrace.

Grief Untold

My heart is heavy with a grief untold,
A burden of sorrow that I can't hold.
The darkness shrouds me in its embrace,
A silent sorrow no one can trace.
The world around me has grown so cold,
My life has turned to one of grey hues.
The darkness has wrapped me in its cloak,
And I'm alone in my blues.
My life is but a shadow of its past,
A dream that slowly fades away.
The light of hope has long since died,
And I'm left in the dark to stay.
The night will linger 'til the dawn,
But my soul will never be the same.
The darkness has taken my heart and soul,
Leaving me in its eternal flame.

The Foundation of Life

The foundation of life is built with care,
    Brick by brick, with love and truth in hand.
    It stands the test of time, it's always there,
    A steadfast guide in a changing land.
    It holds us up, it gives us strength to cope,
    With life's challenges and its endless strife,
    It's always there to help us find a way,
    And shine a light through the storm of life.
    The foundation of life is love and peace,
    It brings us joy and happiness untold,
    It teaches us to be kind and to release,
    The anger, hate and fear that often hold.
    So let us build our lives upon this truth,
    And cherish it as the greatest of our youth.

Pedantic Machismo

Pedantic machismo, a facade so grand,
A false sense of power, in a weak man's hand.
A show of dominance, a need to control,
A mask of bravado, that takes its toll.
A narrow mind, that refuses to see,
The flaws in its own masculinity.
A constant need, to prove oneself,
A never-ending cycle, of one's own hell.
A rigid code, of what a man should be,
A limiting belief, that holds one's free.
Insecurities, hidden behind bravado,
A facade, that will surely erode.
For true strength, lies in vulnerability,
In the courage to admit one's fallibility.
Pedantic machismo, is but a show,
True strength is found in letting go.

Infinity and I

Infinity and I, a journey so vast,
    A path that's endless, that's always fast.
    It's a journey of endlessness, and of wonders so great,
    Infinity and I, a journey that's late.
    It's a journey of mystery, and of secrets untold,
    Infinity and I, a journey that's old.
    It's a journey of endlessness, and of wonders so true,
    Infinity and I, a journey that's new.
    It's a journey of wonder, and of mysteries so deep,
    Infinity and I, a journey that's steep.
    It's a journey of endlessness, and of wonders so great,
    Infinity and I, a journey that's late.
    So, I take this journey, with a heart that's true,
    Infinity and I, a journey that's new.
    A path that's endless, brimming with vitality,
    Infinity and I, a journey of peaceful serenity.

This Is a New Day

This is a new day,
    This is a new day for you.
    This is a new day for my friends.
    This is a new day for the world.
    This is a new day for me.
    This is a new day for my friends.
    I'm never gonna let you go.
    'Cause you came from so far away.
    I always loved you, and now you're walking back.
    But the feeling is that it's right back inside of me.
    Cause you came from so far away.
    And I believe if I get those worries lined up with your head.
    You know I will love you too, yes, I will.
    This is a new day,
    This is a new day for me.
    This is a new day for my friends.
    This is a new day for my friends.

This Is a New Day

This is a new day,
    This is a new day for you.
    This is a new day for my friends.
    This is a new day for the world.
    This is a new day for me.
    This is a new day for my friends,
    I'm never gonna let you go.
    'Cause you came from so far away.
    I always loved you, and now you're walking back.
    But the feeling is that it's right back inside of me.
    Cause you came from so far away.
    And I believe if I get those worries lined up with your head.
    You know I will love you too, yes, I will,
    This is a new day,
    This is a new day for me.
    This is a new day for my friends.
    This is a new day for my friends.

Don't Know How to Begin

All the world needs is lots of love,
    OH, there's a fire outside my heart,
    So, my world's in a funny place
    I'm in a cloud,
    But clouds are clouds that I'm in
    There's a spark and it ain't pretty good enough,
    All I really mean is I'm in a crazy place,
    Can't get a message through,
    And your heart is all in a row, my love,
    That's a hard, hard way, a hard way,
    Oh, but all I really mean is I'm in a crazy place,
    Don't know how to begin,
    All I really mean is I'm in a crazy place,
    Don't know how to begin,
    All I really mean is I'm in a crazy place,
    I heard the news,
    There's been a change,
    And so, amount the time right.

To Be Together

In the shadows of the stars
    Oh, and it's the first time in a very long time,
    Pretty sure I've felt it before
    Let's just take the chance,
    To be together
    One day at a time
    I just don't understand,
    The feeling it is having, while you're young.
    Another thing a long time gone by
    Pretty sure I'm feeling this way,
    Pretty sure I have to say,
    Everything can be turned on their minds,
    I just no longer notice,
    If 'cause you're beautiful
    Tell me how can, I know you do,
    I just wonder would you stay if,
    Today is the day my time starts,
    Suddenly fading away
    Wake up, it's almost like this,
    Please wake up or it's nine in the morning,
    People can hurt you, but not me.

Bold Ink

Inked in bold and vivid hues,
A canvas of her body she chooses.
The colors bold and vibrant seen,
A story of her life within.
A tribute, a memorial, a reminder too,
Of who she has been and what she'll do.
The ink a reminder of her past,
Her future she creates, her present she'll last.
The tattoos her story, her life, her fate,
Her rebellion, her strength, her will not to break.
The ink a reminder of the woman she's become,
A warrior of life, her courage the sum.
The tattoos her armor, her shield and her sword,
A reminder of her strength, her courage restored.
Ink her body, her spirit, her soul,
A story of courage, of strength and of bold.

The Whole Country Is Asleep

The whole country is asleep,
    And you'd better come and come from me,
    All that you got is all that I had to give,
    The whole country is asleep,
    I'm a guilty gentleman,
    I'm just another man to everybody else,
    But I've built it up one,
    You know that I can't be easily swayed,
    You know that I've been here a very, very long time,
    And if you want it, you can try,
    But I've built it up one,
    And the whole country is asleep,
    And you'd better come and come from me,
    Oh, baby, baby,
    I've got a list of names,
    And if you want it, you can buy it,
    You know I'm not trying to be,
    There seems like an invisible line,
    Baby, baby, more faces.

I Feel a Monster

I feel a monster stirring deep within my soul,
    A creature of darkness, an ever-growing hole.
    It lurks in the shadows and feeds on my pain,
    Forever lurking, never to be slain.
    It gnaws at my heart, its power so strong,
    My courage is tested, but I won't be wronged.
    It's a force of destruction, a darkness that creeps,
    It swallows my spirit, my soul it keeps.
    As I battle this monster, with all my might,
    I know I can win this; I must put up a fight.
    For this creature can't take me, no matter the cost,
    I will never surrender, no matter the loss.
    I will fight this beast, I will be strong,
    For I know that I'm worth, I'm where I belong.
    My will is unbreakable, my courage will last,
    This monster in me, it will not surpass.

In the End

The end of a relationship,
It's a pain like no other,
It's a feeling of loss,
It's a feeling of doubt.
The memories that haunt me,
They play like a movie reel,
The love that we shared,
It's a love that I still feel.
The end of a relationship,
It's a change that I didn't choose,
It's a change that I fear,
It's a change that I can't lose.
The loneliness that surrounds me,
It's a feeling that I can't shake,
The end of a relationship,
It's a heartache.
But I'll pick up the pieces,
I'll mend my broken heart,
I'll move on from this pain,
I'll find a new start.

Wake Up with Determination

Wake up with determination,
Go to bed with satisfaction,
That's the secret, to a fulfilling day,
That's the key, to a contented way.
Wake up with determination,
Go to bed with satisfaction,
Set your goals, and make a plan,
Work hard and take a stand.
Wake up with determination,
Go to bed with satisfaction,
Don't let setbacks, or failures, stop you,
Don't let doubts, or fears, fool you.
Wake up with determination,
Go to bed with satisfaction,
Keep going, and keep striving,
Keep believing and keep thriving.
For wake up with determination
Go to bed with satisfaction,
That's the secret, to a fulfilling day,
That's the key, to a contented way.

Our Dreams Can Come True

All our dreams, can come true, if we have, the courage, to pursue them,
That's the truth, that's timeless, and universal, and real
With a belief, that's unshakable, and unwavering, and unshakable
With a hope, that's unshakable, and unwavering, and unshakable.
All our dreams, can come true, if we have, the courage, to pursue them,
That's the promise, that's enduring, and empowering, and inspiring
With a heart, that's full, and open, and receptive
With a mind, that's open, and receptive, and inquisitive.
All our dreams, can come true, if we have, the courage, to pursue them,
That's the message, that's uplifting, and motivating, and inspiring
With a spirit, that's determined, and resilient, and undaunted
With a soul, that's determined, and resilient, and undaunted.
So, don't give up, on your dreams, or your hopes, or your aspirations
Don't give up, on your vision, or your goals, or your ambitions,
Don't give up, on your potential, or your abilities, or your talents,
Don't give up, on your worth, or your value, or your dignity.
For all our dreams, can come true, if we have, the courage, to pursue them,
That's the truth, that's timeless, and universal, and real
With a belief, that's unshakable, and unwavering, and unshakable
With a hope, that's unshakable, and unwavering, and unshakable.

A Man of Mystery

A man of mystery, and power
    Whose power, is exceeded, only by his mystery,
    A man of secrets, and strength
    Whose strength is matched, only by his secrets.
    A man of mystery, and power
    Whose power, is shrouded, in enigma and intrigue,
    A man of riddles, and might
    Whose might is veiled, in mystery and might.
    A man of mystery, and power
    Whose power, is feared, and respected, and admired,
    A man of puzzles, and force
    Whose force is admired, and feared, and respected.
    So, don't underestimate, the mystery, of this man,
    Don't underestimate, the power, of this man,
    Don't underestimate, the secrets, of this man,
    Don't underestimate, the strength, of this man.
    For a man of mystery, and power
    Whose power, is exceeded, only by his mystery,
    A man of secrets, and strength
    Whose strength is matched, only by his secrets.

Children of the Fog

Children of the fog, a world so misty,
    A place of magic, that's always busy.
    It's a world of mystery, and of secrets untold,
    Children of the fog, a place that's old.
    It's a world of magic, and of wonders so true,
    Children of the fog, a place that's new.
    It's a world of mystery, and of secrets so deep,
    Children of the fog, a place that's steep.
    It's a world of wonder, and of magic so great,
    Children of the fog, a place that's late.
    It's a world of mystery, and of secrets untold,
    Children of the fog, a place that's old.
    So, I stand before it, with a heart that's true,
    Children of the fog, a place that's new.
    A world of magic, alive with energy,
    Children of the fog, a place of serenity.

The Clock is Ticking

The clock is ticking, time is short,
    I must write this poem, with all my might,
    The words flow fast, like a rushing stream,
    My pen can't keep up, it's a race to the finish line.
    I weave and dodge, through the tangled words,
    My mind is racing, my heart is pumping,
    I must capture the essence, the feeling, the emotion,
    In just a few short lines, it's a marathon, not a sprint.
    I don't have time to stop and ponder,
    I must keep going, until the end
    I pour out my soul, my heart, my passion,
    Into this poem, my dearest friend.
    And as the clock strikes midnight
    I lay down my pen, with a sigh of relief,
    I did it, I conquered the clock,
    My poem is done, and so am I.

The Slow Progress of Entropy

The slow progress of entropy,
    A creeping, insidious force.
It eats away at everything,
    Leaving nothing but a scorched earth.
It starts with just a tiny crack,
    A small imperfection in the veneer.
But over time, it grows and spreads,
    Until everything is laid bare and clear.
It doesn't discriminate,
    It doesn't care about your status or your wealth.
It takes and takes and takes,
    Until there's nothing left.
But we keep fighting against it,
    We keep trying to hold on.
We rebuild and restore,
    Hoping that we can live on.
So, let's embrace the slow progress of entropy,
    And all the challenges it brings.
For in the end, it makes us stronger,
    And it helps us spread our wings.

The World Awakens
    The morning dew, it sparkles bright,
    Bright, like a thousand diamonds on the ground.
    The grass, it glistens in the light,
    Light, that filters through the trees all around.
    The birds, they sing their joyous song,
    Song, that fills the air with melodies.

The world awakens, all along,
Along, the path that leads to destiny.
The sun, it rises in the sky,
Sky, that stretches on without an end.
I take a deep breath, and let out a sigh,
Sigh, of gratitude for this new day to spend.
I am alive, and I am free,
Free, to explore and find my way.
Each day, a new adventure for me,
Me, to discover and enjoy.

The Memories Remain

The autumn leaves, they fall so gently,
Gently, to the ground below.
Their vibrant hues, a sight so splendid,
Splendid, as the wind begins to blow.
The air is crisp, the skies are clear,
Clear, as far as the eye can see.
I wander through this tranquil scene,
Scene, of natural beauty.
The sun, it sets behind the trees,
Trees, that stand so tall and proud.
I pause to take it all in,
In, this peaceful, serene crowd.
The dizain may be coming to an end,
End, but the memories, they remain.
I'll hold them close, and cherish them,
Them, until we meet again.

Bad Example

I'm not totally useless,
    You can always use me, as a bad example
I may not be perfect, or the best,
But I can still, be useful, in some ways, and ample.
I'm not totally useless,
You can always use me, as a cautionary tale
I may not be the role model, or the standard,
But I can still, teach you, something, that will prevail.
I'm not totally useless,
You can always use me, as a reference point
I may not be the guide, or the mentor,
But I can still, show you, something, that will anoint.
So, don't dismiss me, or my value,
Don't dismiss me, or my worth,
Don't dismiss me, or my potential,
Don't dismiss me, or my mirth.
For I'm not totally useless
You can always use me, as a bad example
I may not be perfect, or the best,
But I can still, be useful, in some ways, and ample.

Coffee and Confidence

Coffee in one hand, confidence in another
That's the way, I start my day,
With a boost, of caffeine, and a boost, of self-assurance
With a lift, of energy, and a lift, of self-persuasion.
Coffee in one hand, confidence in another
That's the way, I tackle the world,
With a shot, of courage, and a shot, of conviction
With a spark, of determination, and a spark, of affliction.
Coffee in one hand, confidence in another
That's the way, I face my fears,
With a swig, of strength, and a swig, of resolve
With a gulp, of fortitude, and a gulp, of absolve.
So, don't underestimate me, or my power,
Don't underestimate me, or my might,
Don't underestimate me, or my spirit,
Don't underestimate me, or my light.
For coffee in one hand, confidence in another
That's the way, I start my day,
With a boost, of caffeine, and a boost, of self-assurance
With a lift, of energy, and a lift, of self-persuasion.

I Want To Lose My Soul

I want to go into the dark.
    I want to get off of my own phone.
    I want to get off of my own mind.
    So, I can be the man for me.
    I can be that girl for me.
    I want to go through the motions.
    I want to lose my soul.
    I want to lose my touch.
    I want to get off my own phone.
    So, I can be the man for me.
    So I can be that girl for me.
    I want to go through the motions.
    I want to lose my soul.
    I want to lose my touch.
    I want to get off of my own phone.
    So, I can be the man for me.
    I can be that girl for me.
    I want to go through the motions.
    I want to lose my soul.
    I want to lose my touch.

Throwing Kindness Around

Throwing kindness, around, like confetti
That's the way, I am, and that's the way, I'll be.
With a heart, that's full, and open, and generous
With a soul, that's kind, and compassionate, and generous
Throwing kindness, around, like confetti
That's the way, I live, and that's the way, I thrive.
With a spirit, that's joyous, and cheerful, and light
With a mind, that's joyful, and cheerful, and light
Throwing kindness, around, like confetti
That's the way, I give, and that's the way, I share
With a gesture, that's small, but meaningful, and thoughtful
With a touch, that's thoughtful, and meaningful, and small
So don't be afraid, to show kindness, or to give kindness, or to share kindness
Don't be afraid, to spread love, or to spread joy, or to spread light
Don't be afraid, to be yourself, or to be genuine, or to be authentic
Don't be afraid, to be kind, or to be compassionate, or to be generous!

Love Starts Within

Self-love is a journey,
A path we must travel alone.
It's a journey of discovery,
Of finding out who we are on our own.
It's a journey of acceptance,
Of learning to embrace our flaws.
It's a journey of forgiveness,
Of letting go of the past and all it holds.
It's a journey of self-care,
Of taking time for ourselves each day.
It's a journey of compassion,
Of loving ourselves in every single way.
Self-love is a journey,
A journey worth taking each day.
It's the path to happiness,
And the key to living in a brighter, more loving way.

Side-Effect

Weird is a side-effect of awesome,
    A quirk of the truly unique.
    It's the mark of those who dare to be different,
    Who refuse to be mundane and meek.
    Weird is a sign of creativity,
    A mark of a curious mind.
    It's the trait of those who think outside the box,
    Who are one-of-a-kind, one of a kind.
    Weird is a blessing, not a curse,
    A badge of honor, not a shame.
    It's the mark of those who embrace their quirks,
    Who play by their own rules and claim.
    Their place in this world as their own.
    So, embrace your weirdness with pride,
    For it is a sign of your awesomeness,
    A mark of the extraordinary inside.

I Can't Pretend

I'm not a fool.
I can't pretend.
That I don't need you
And maybe you'll understand.
But you're not that.
Unrequited love
That's the curse of everyone.
Trying to help it rid the world of you.
Let me know!
That's not really what this is all about
I'm not a fool.
I can't pretend.
That I don't need you
I'm so afraid of your love.
I'm not what you look like
I'm not what you could be.
I'm not what you want me to be.
I'm not what you would come be mine
I'm not what you'd call a ""sick man.""
I'm not what you'd call a ""sick man.""

You Better Do Something

In my mind
    We can do it.
    It's not much of a surprise.
    I don't mind a thing.
    So, what is it we're gonna do?
    What does it mean to you?
    Well, it's not that I don't love ya!
    I think we're just gonna waste my time (overshot)
    It's just that after all (overshot)
    I've wasted my time (overshot)
    I've wasted my time.
    I'm not gonna waste my time.
    Yeah, hey there's people out there.
    Hey there's people out there!
    Hey there's people out there!
    You gotta do something, do something, chick you gotta do something.
    Yeah, you gotta do something.
    yeah, you gotta do something.
    You better do something.
    You better do something.

Five Days

The first five days after the weekend
    Are always the hardest, it's true.
    It's a struggle, to get back into the swing
    Of things, and to face the week anew.
    The freedom and relaxation, of the weekend
    Is hard to let go, and to forget.
    It's tough, to get back into the grind
    And to face the challenges, that we must yet.
    But we push through, and we persevere.
    We find the strength, to carry on
    We put one foot in front of the other
    And we face the week, head on.
    For the first five days after the weekend
    Are always the hardest, but we'll get through.
    We'll find a way, to keep moving forward.
    And we'll make it, to the weekend, anew.

The Mournful Wind's Song

The moon, a goddess, rules the starry night,
Her silver light a guide for those astray.
The ancient trees, with leaves of green and bright,
Bow down to her, in honor and in sway.
The wind, a spirit, sings a mournful tune,
A song of magic, ancient and unknown.
The wildflowers, with petals soft as moon,
Dance to the beat, their beauty fully shown.
The earth, a mother, nurtures all within,
A source of life, a shelter from the storm.
Her breath, a breeze, a caress of kin,
A loving touch, a constant and a norm.
The pagan path, a journey rich and true,
A connection to the world, old and new.

That's What I'm Talking About

And you know how it feels.
    You're my fire.
    You know what I mean.
    You've got my love.
    My love
    My love, my love, love
    That's what I'm talking about
    My love, my love, love
    That's what I'm talking about
    My love, my love, love, love
    That's what I'm talking about, that's what I'm talking about
    Love, love, love, love, love
    Love is sweet.
    Love is good enough.
    Love is wasted.
    Love cuts you with love.
    Love, love, love
    That's what I'm talking about
    Love, love, love, love, love
    That's what I'm talking about
    My love, my love, love, love.

When I'm Alone

It doesn't mean I'm lonely, when I'm alone
 I can find peace in the quiet, the unknown
 It's a time to recharge, to be with myself
 To reflect and ponder, to seek some kind of wealth
 In the thoughts and feelings that bubble up inside
 It doesn't mean I'm lonely, when I'm alone.
 I can find joy in solitude, and let go.
 Of the noise and chaos that surrounds me
 It's a chance to breathe and be free.
 To discover who I am, and what I need.
 It doesn't mean I'm lonely, when I'm alone
 It's a chance to be strong, and stand on my own
 To embrace my independence, and be at peace
 It doesn't mean I'm lonely, when I'm alone.
 It's a time to be whole and find my way home.

Bang My Head

I bang my head against walls
>To bring words out, to make them fall.
>From the depths of my mind, where they're trapped and stuck.
>I bang and bang, trying to unlock
>The gates that keep them hidden away
>I bang and bang, hoping to say,
>What's in my heart, what's on my mind.
>I bang and bang, trying to find,
>The right way to express myself.
>I bang and bang, seeking some kind of wealth.
>In the words that finally escape
>I bang my head against walls, it's a desperate
>Attempt to communicate and be heard!
>I bang and bang, hoping a single word
>Will finally break free and set me free.
>I bang my head against walls, it's the only way I can be me.

The Path to Clarity

The path to clarity is a winding road,
That twists and turns, with obstacles ahead,
But if we follow truth, we'll reach our goal,
And find a life filled with peace and no regret.
It's not always easy, and we may stray,
But truth is always there to lead us back,
It shows us what is real, it lights the way,
And brings us clarity, a new life track.
For truth is like a beacon, shining bright,
In a world that often seems so dark and dim,
It guides us through the shadows of the night,
And gives us hope for a brighter tomorrow win.
So let us hold truth close, and never fear,
For it will lead us to the path of clarity clear.

The Vibes and the Rhymes

I feel the vibes, and the rhymes,
 A rhythm that's inside, that always shines.
 It courses through my veins, and fills my soul,
 A rhythm that's alive, and always whole.
 I feel the vibes, and the rhymes,
 A magic that's within, that always climbs.
 It lifts me up, and carries me away,
 A rhythm that's alive, and always stays.
 I feel the vibes, and the rhymes,
 A music that's inside, that always chimes.
 It speaks to me, and fills my heart,
 A rhythm that's alive, and never parts.
 So, I dance to the vibes, and the rhymes,
 A rhythm that's inside, that always climbs.
 I let it take me, and carry me away,
 A rhythm that's alive, and always stays.

Being Unique

I'm unique, just like everyone else.
    We all have our quirks and our quirks to dwell
    On the things that make us who we are
    I'm unique, just like everyone else.
    We all have our stories, and our stories to tell
    Of the journey that brought us this far
    I'm unique, just like everyone else.
    We all have our struggles, and our struggles to overcome
    To find our place in the world, and become
    The best version of ourselves that we can be.
    I'm unique, just like everyone else
    We all have our talents, and our talents to see
    The gifts that we have, and how we can use them
    I'm unique, just like everyone else.
    We all have the potential, to be something great,
    To make our mark on the world, and create
    A life that's meaningful and true.
    I'm unique, just like everyone else
    We all have the power, to be something more
    To embrace our individuality, and explore
    The wonders that life has in store.

Dark Journey

Embrace the dead, a journey so dark,
A path of darkness, that's always stark.
It's a journey of death, and of secrets untold,
Embrace the dead, a path that's old.
It's a journey of darkness, and of shadows so deep,
Embrace the dead, a path that's steep.
It's a journey of death, and of wonders so great,
Embrace the dead, a path that's late.
It's a journey of terror, and of danger so real,
Embrace the dead, a path that's zeal.
It's a journey of death, and of secrets so true,
Embrace the dead, a path that's new.
So, I stand before it, with a heart that's true,
Embrace the dead, a path that's new.
A journey through death, full of vitality,
Embracing the deceased, a path of harmony.

Chaos Party

It was a party like no other,
    A chaotic, wild affair.
    People were dancing on the tables,
    And the music was blasting through the air.
    There was laughter and shouting,
    As the night wore on.
    Everyone was having a blast,
    And no one wanted the party to be gone.
    But as the hours ticked by,
    The chaos reached a fever pitch.
    People were stumbling and falling,
    As the room began to glitch.
    It was a mess, a disaster,
    But somehow, we all survived.
    And as the sun began to rise,
    We knew that we had truly thrived.
    So, let's raise a glass to the chaos,
    And the memories that we made.
    For the chaos party will always be,
    A night that we'll never forget or evade.

Descent Into Madness

A descent into madness,
A spiral of despair,
A loss of self and sanity,
Beyond repair.
The voices in my head,
They scream and shout,
They twist my thoughts,
And wear my mind out.
The walls close in,
The darkness grows,
I'm suffocating,
No one knows.
I'm trapped in this hell,
This mental abyss,
I'm drowning in madness,
I can't resist.
A descent into madness,
A fall from grace,
I've lost myself,
I can't escape.

Seeking Respect

Seeking respect, not attention
　For it lasts longer, and means more,
　Attention is fleeting, and often shallow,
　But respect is earned, and well-deserved.
　It's not about seeking the spotlight,
　But about being true to yourself
　It's not about seeking approval,
　But about earning it, through hard work and dedication.
　Respect is something that's built over time,
　It's not something that's given, or taken lightly
　It's earned through honesty, and integrity,
　And it's something that's valued and held dear.
　So, don't seek attention, for its own sake,
　But instead, strive for respect, and all it entails,
　For it will last longer, and be more fulfilling,
　And it will bring you true happiness, and joy.

Flame-Haired Goddess

A redhaired beauty queen, with locks of flame,
Her eyes, like emeralds, sparkle and gleam.
Her smile, a ray of sunshine, lights up the scene,
A goddess among mere mortals, she seems.
Her beauty, beyond compare, radiates,
A fire in her soul, a passion that shines.
She walks with grace and power, she captivates,
Her presence, a gift, a blessing divine.
She rules with kindness, a heart full of love,
Her laughter, a melody, sweet and pure.
Her spirit, a flame that burns from above,
Her essence, a treasure, forever endure.
So, here's to the redhaired beauty queen,
A gem among the rough, a sight serene.
May she reign supreme, her reign evergreen,
A symbol of beauty, grace, and self-esteem.

Seize the Day

Every day brings, an opportunity, to do something legendary,
    It's a chance, to make a mark, and to shine,
    It's a chance, to be bold, and to be brave,
    It's a chance, to make a difference, and to intertwine.
    Every day brings, an opportunity, to do something legendary,
    It's a chance, to be remembered, and to be revered
    It's a chance, to inspire, and to be admired
    It's a chance, to be a hero, and to be cleared.
    Every day brings, an opportunity, to do something legendary
    It's a chance, to live your dream, and to make it real
    It's a chance, to leave a legacy, and to seal
    It's a chance, to be great, and to feel.
    So, seize the day, and make it count
    Seize the day, and do your best,
    Seize the day, and be remarkable,
    Seize the day and be impressed.
    For every day brings, an opportunity, to do something legendary,
    It's a chance, to make a mark, and to shine,
    It's a chance, to be bold, and to be brave,
    It's a chance, to make a difference, and to intertwine.

Start A Fire

I'm gonna start a charity cause.
There's nothing that I wouldn't do.
I'm gonna give back everything I can.
I'm gonna get to know someone.
And start a fire.
I'm gonna try my best to make them mine
I'm gonna get to know someone.
And start a fire.
I'm gonna try my best to make them mine
I'm gonna get to know someone.
And start a fire.
I'm gonna try my best to make them mine
I'm gonna get to know someone.
And start a fire.
I'm gonna try my best to make them mine
When did we all wake up so early?
When did we all let the carpet down?
We rode in caravans alone.

Dreaming Bigger

Dreaming bigger, than my imagination, can handle,
That's the way, I live my life,
With a vision, that's boundless, and limitless
With a dream, that's fearless, and tireless.
Dreaming bigger, than my imagination, can handle,
That's the way, I set my goals,
With a plan, that's ambitious, and audacious
With a desire, that's relentless, and spacious.
Dreaming bigger, than my imagination, can handle,
That's the way, I pursue my dreams
With a passion, that's burning, and intense
With a drive, that's unstoppable, and immense.
So don't limit, your dreams, or your aspirations
Don't limit, your vision, or your scope,
Don't limit, your potential, or your possibilities
Don't limit, your ambition, or your hope.
For dreaming bigger, than your imagination, can handle,
That's the way, to live a life, that's full
With a vision, that's boundless, and limitless
With a dream, that's fearless, and tireless.

Within and Without Reflect Each Other

Within and without reflect each other,
    Like two sides of the same coin.
    What lies within us shapes our outer selves,
    And what we show to the world reflects our inner joy or turmoil.
    Our thoughts and feelings influence our actions,
    And our actions shape our reality.
    So, if we want to change the world around us,
    We must first start by changing ourselves within.
    We are constantly evolving,
    Growing and changing with each passing day.
    And as we work to better ourselves,
    We can't help but radiate a positive energy that touches everyone
we encounter.
    So, let's strive to be our best selves,
    Both within and without.
    For as we work to improve ourselves,
    We can't help but create a better world, no doubt.

Bad Choices Make Good Stories

Bad choices make good stories,
>They may not be the best, or the wisest, or the most thoughtful
>But they are the ones, that we remember, and that we talk about
>They are the ones, that we laugh at, and that we share.
>Bad choices make good stories,
>They may not be the ones, that we proud of, or that we boast
>But they are the ones, that we learn from, and that we grow
>They are the ones, that we reflect on, and that we regret.
>Bad choices make good stories,
>They may not be the ones, that we recommend, or that we endorse
>But they are the ones, that we experience, and that we live
>They are the ones, that we embrace, and that we forgive.
>So, don't shy away, from your mistakes,
>Don't shy away, from your mishaps,
>Don't shy away, from your blunders,
>Don't shy away, from your flaps.
>For bad choices make good stories
>They may not be the best, or the wisest, or the most thoughtful,
>But they are the ones, that we remember, and that we talk about
>They are the ones, that we laugh at, and that we share.

House Full of Flowers

I woke up this morning, to a house full of flowers,
    In every room, in every shower.
    I couldn't believe it, it was such a surprise,
    A riot of color, before my very eyes.
    I wandered from room to room, in awe and delight,
    The flowers were blooming, in the morning light.
    I couldn't help but smile, at this strange, odd sight,
    A house full of flowers, such a beautiful, wondrous sight.
    I don't know how it happened, or who is to blame,
    But I'll enjoy the flowers, while they remain.
    I'll dance and sing, and bask in their glow,
    A house full of flowers, how could I not know.
    This would be my day, such a strange, odd way.

In the Dark of Night

In the dark of night, when all is still,
    And shadows dance upon the walls,
    I lie awake and ponder, at will,
    The mysteries and sorrows that befall.
    The world is full of pain and strife,
    Of heartache, loss, and grief,
    And yet we try to go on with life,
    To find some solace, some relief.
    But in the darkness, all is clear,
    The doubts and fears that haunt the day,
    The secrets whispered in the ear,
    The doubts that steal our joy away.
    So let me rest in this dark sonnet,
    And dream of happier days ahead,
    For even in the night, there is a chance,
    That sunlight will once more be shed.

Paul McCartney Love Songs

Oh, the love songs of Paul McCartney,
They sing to my heart and soul.
They lift me up when I'm feeling down,
And make me feel whole.
His voice is like a soothing balm,
A gentle and tender sound.
It fills me with a sense of peace,
And lifts my feet off the ground.
His lyrics speak of love and hope,
Of dreams and second chances.
They remind me that anything is possible,
And love can conquer all advances.
So, here's to Paul McCartney,
And his beautiful love songs.
They've brought joy and comfort,
To me and countless others, all along.

Do Small Things in a Great Way

If you can't do great things, do small things in a great way
That's the secret, to making a difference.
That's the key, to leaving a mark,
That's the way, to being a presence,
If you can't do great things, do small things in a great way,
That's the secret, to making an impact.
That's the key, to making a change,
That's the way, to being intact.
If you can't do great things, do small things in a great way
That's the secret, to making a contribution.
That's the key, to making a difference
That's the way, to making a resolution.
So don't underestimate, the power, of small things
Don't underestimate, the impact, of little deeds.
Don't underestimate, the value, of simple acts,
Don't underestimate, the worth, of your deeds.
For if you can't do great things, do small things in a great way
That's the secret, to making a difference.
That's the key, to leaving a mark,
That's the way, to being a presence.

Goes 'Round And Around

I'm just waiting on a special someone.
Goes 'round and around.
Taking my time, I'm looking at all the stares.
But I'm not asking for your love and trust.
And the lines are blurry and they're closing in
I'm just waiting on a special someone.
Goes 'round and around.
Taking my time and I'm looking at all the stares.
But I'm not asking for your love and trust.
And the lines are blurry and they're closing in
I'm just waiting on a special someone.
Goes 'round and around.
Taking my time and I'm looking at all the stares.
But I'm not asking for your love and trust.
And the lines are blurry and they're closing in
I'm just waiting on a special someone.
Goes 'round and around.

With Her

That I wish
  I've got my reasons; I won't try to understand.
  But to me, my reasons
  I believe, at least I know.
  That I would be content
  To spend my whole life with her
  And for now, I'll only spend my life along.
  She's there for me.
  And she is the one.
  She's there for me.
  I believe I would be content.
  To spend my whole life with her
  And for now, I'll only spend my life along.
  With her
  With her
  With her
  You know you're the one.
  You're my only one.
  And yet, with her, my number one
  And I know, with her, her heart's my savior.
  Tell the whole world I'm alright!
  I know, and you're not even there.

Where Cold Faces Dwell

There is a place where cold faces dwell,
Where emotions are locked away.
Where smiles are rare and laughter's scarce,
And no one dares to stray.
It's a place of icy silence,
Where hearts are made of stone.
Where love and warmth and kindness,
Are things that are unknown.
But in the midst of all this cold,
There's a glimmer of hope within.
For even in the darkest of places,
The light of love can still begin.
So don't be afraid to venture,
To the place where cold faces dwell.
For with a little bit of courage,
You can break the icy spell.

Divine Love Triangle

It was a love triangle of the divine,
    A dance of three celestial beings.
    Each one shining bright,
    Their love a light that was searing.
    There was the sun, the bright and bold,
    The one who shone the brightest.
    He was fierce and passionate,
    And his love knew no limit.
    There was the moon, the ethereal one,
    Whose love was gentle and kind.
    She was a mystery, a mystery,
    And her love was hard to find.
    And then there was the earth,
    The one who was caught in between.
    She loved them both, in different ways,
    And her love was a tapestry of green.
    It was a love triangle of the divine,
    A dance of three celestial beings.
    And though it was a complex love,
    It was a love that was worth seeing.

Darkness of Depression

The darkness of depression,
    It surrounds me like a cloak,
    It weighs me down,
    It chokes.
    The thoughts that plague me,
    They twist and they turn,
    They fill me with self-hatred,
    They make my spirit burn.
    The motivation that once was,
    It's faded away,
    The energy that I had,
    It's gone astray.
    The darkness of depression,
    It consumes me whole,
    It drains me of life,
    It takes its toll.
    The joy that I knew,
    It's a distant memory,
    The darkness of depression,
    It's all I can see.

Feral Generation

We are the feral generation,
Raised on the streets and in the shadows.
We've learned to survive in a world of chaos,
Where only the strong and the cunning make it through.
We don't follow the rules of society,
We forge our own path and make our own way.
We live for the thrill of the moment,
And never look back on the past or the future.
We are the wild ones, the misfits, the rebels.
We don't fit in with the mainstream.
But we don't care, because we know,
That we are stronger together than we ever could be alone.
We are the feral generation,
And we won't be tamed or controlled.
We'll roam free and live life on our own terms,
Until the end of time.

Just Wanna Hold On

You can only try so hard.
　　You're gonna make your daddy wait.
　　So, if he ever calls
　　Or the day is over and you've moved on
　　Can you count the things he doesn't wanna say
　　Tell him how much he loves to see him play
　　Cause you're alone and that's how you get him
　　Just wanna hold on.
　　Kiss him, baby, that's what he wants to know.
　　Hold on, baby, that's what he wants to know
　　That's what he wants to know.
　　That's what he wants to know.
　　Baby, that's what he wants to know.
　　That's what he's getting excited about
　　Baby, baby, that's what he wants to know.
　　Wait (that's what he wants to know)
　　Wait (that's what he wants to know)

Tomb of the Old Gods

In a forgotten land, where time stands still,
There lies a tomb, where the old gods rest,
Their power once mighty, now lies dormant still,
Their spirits lost, in a never-ending quest.
It's said that they once ruled with iron hand,
With powers beyond what mere mortals could grasp,
But now they lay buried, in this foreign land,
Their legacy fading, a memory of the past.
The tomb is grand, with pillars tall and proud,
And carvings etched in stone, with tales untold,
Of battles won and lost, of love, and of vows,
Of a time when gods walked amongst the bold.
So let us pay our respects to the old gods,
For they have given us stories to unfold.

50/50 Balance

50% savage, 50% sweetness
    That's the balance, of my soul.
    50% fire, 50% ice,
    That's the balance, that makes me whole.
    50% wild, 50% tame
    That's the balance, of my heart.
    50% fierce, 50% kind
    That's the balance, that sets me apart.
    50% rebel, 50% rule follower
    That's the balance, of my mind.
    50% risk taker, 50% careful
    That's the balance, that I find.
    So, don't judge me, by just one side.
    Don't judge me, by just one part.
    There's more to me, than meets the eye,
    There's more to me, than just one art.
    For I am 50% savage, 50% sweetness,
    I am a balance, of fire and ice.
    I am 50% wild, 50% tame,
    I am a balance, of fierce and nice.
    I am 50% rebel, 50% rule follower,
    I am a balance, of risk and care.
    I am 50% savage, 50% sweetness,
    I am a balance, that's unique, and rare.

Ode to Eris

Eris, goddess of discord and strife,
Your name is whispered in the night.
You bring chaos and confusion,
But also, the spark of new solutions.
With your golden apple in hand,
You stir up trouble in this land.
You challenge the status quo,
And force us to think and grow.
But your power is not to be feared,
For without you, we'd be stuck in the mire.
You push us to face our fears,
And to overcome the doubts and tears.
So, here's an ode to you, Eris,
Goddess of chaos and surprise.
You may cause us some distress,
But without you, life would be less.

The Timeless Path

We live in yesterday's tomorrow,
　A place where time is never hollow.
　Memories of yesterday, visions of today,
　Hopes and dreams for what's yet to come our way.
　The future is a mystery, a path untold,
　A journey we must take, as we grow old.
　Yesterday's lessons, tomorrow's plans,
　Guide us on our way, with open hands.
　The past is our foundation, a foundation strong,
　A guide to what we've been, what we've done wrong.
　The future is a promise, a path to follow,
　A journey that begins, with each tomorrow.
　So let us cherish yesterday, embrace today,
　And look to tomorrow, with hope and pray.
　For we live in yesterday's tomorrow,
　A place where time is never hollow.

I'm Not Your Superman

I'm not your superman, I'm just a man,
　　With flaws and imperfections, like everyone,
　　I have my own struggles, my own plan,
　　And I face them all with courage, not a ton.
　　I can't fly, I can't save the world alone,
　　I can't make your troubles disappear with ease,
　　But I can be here for you, be a home,
　　And help you find the strength you need to please.
　　I'm not your superman, I can't be all,
　　The things that you might need or want me to be,
　　But I'll stand beside you, through it all,
　　And help you find the happiness you see.
　　So don't put me on a pedestal so high,
　　I'm just a man, doing the best I can,
　　But with your love, and by my side,
　　Together, we'll overcome and take a stand.

I Am Searching

I am searching, for sanity and satire,
    I am seeking, a way to make sense, of this crazy world.
    I am looking, for a way, to find some balance,
    And to bring some light, to the darkness, and the swirl.
    I am searching, for sanity and satire,
    I am hoping, to find some humor, in the chaos.
    I am trying, to find a way, to laugh and cope,
    And to find some joy, in the midst of the hopeless.
    I am searching, for sanity and satire,
    I am longing, for a way to make a difference.
    I am trying, to find a way, to make a mark,
    And to bring some hope, to the indifference.
    So, if you see me, looking lost, or confused,
    Don't judge, or criticize, or refuse.
    Just know, that I am searching, for sanity and satire,
    And that I'm doing my best, to make sense, of this crazy world.

Candle Shrouded in Darkness

A candle shrouded in darkness, a light so small,
    A glimmer of hope, that's standing tall.
    It's a light that's fragile, and full of grace,
    A candle shrouded in darkness, a light that's ablaze.
    It's a light that's shining, in the midst of the night,
    A candle shrouded in darkness, a light that's bright.
    It's a light that's guiding, and leading the way,
    A candle shrouded in darkness, a light that's gay.
    It's a light that's burning, with a fierce and true flame,
    A candle shrouded in darkness, a light that's the same.
    It's a light that's shining, and full of life,
    A candle shrouded in darkness, a light that's rife.
    So I stand before it, with a heart that's true,
    A candle shrouded in darkness, a light that's new.
    A glimmer of hope, that strengthens the heart,
    A candle shrouded in darkness, a light for us from the start.

The Trees are Burned Down to the Ground

The trees are burned down to the ground,
    Their ashes scatter in the breeze.
    Once tall and proud, now reduced to dust,
    Their loss is a sight that does not cease.
    The fire was swift and unforgiving,
    It left a path of destruction in its wake.
    The trees stood no chance against its fury,
    Their leaves and branches all did shake.
    But even as the ashes settle,
    There is a glimmer of hope to be found.
    For from the ashes, new life will emerge,
    And the trees will once again abound.
    So let us mourn the loss of the trees,
    But let us also remember their strength.
    For even in their darkest hour,
    They have the power to regenerate and lengthen.

Distorted Perceptions

In a world of skewed vision,
Where right is left and wrong is right,
It's hard to make a clear decision,
When everything is out of sight.
Our perceptions twist and bend,
Until we can't see straight,
Our thoughts become unhinged,
As we begin to contemplate.
But through the fog and haze,
A glimmer of hope appears,
A chance to break free from the maze,
And face our doubts and fears.
So, let's open up our eyes,
And see things for what they are,
With clear and steady skies,
We can reach for the stars.

I Live vicariously Through Myself

Living vicariously through myself
I see the world through my own eyes.
I experience all the highs and lows,
I live each moment, and never let it go.
I am my own guide, and my own company,
I don't need anyone else, to be happy.
I am content with my own thoughts and feelings,
I live vicariously through myself and find meaning.
In the simple things, and the big adventures
I don't need anyone else, to live a life that's rich and full.
I am my own source of joy and inspiration,
I live vicariously through myself and find satisfaction.
In the way I live, and the way I am.
I don't need anyone else, to validate who I am.
I am comfortable in my own skin,
I live vicariously through myself, and never give in.
To the pressure to be someone else
I am who I am, and that's all I need to be.
I live vicariously through myself, and that's all I need.

A Journey of Evil

Twisted virtues, a path so dark,
  A journey of evil, that's always stark.
  It's a journey of deception, and of secrets untold,
  Twisted virtues, a path that's old.
  It's a journey of wickedness, and of darkness so deep,
  Twisted virtues, a path that's steep.
  It's a journey of evil, and of wonders so great,
  Twisted virtues, a path that's late.
  It's a journey of danger, and of terror so real,
  Twisted virtues, a path that's zeal.
  It's a journey of deception, and of secrets so true,
  Twisted virtues, a path that's new.
  So, I stand before it, with a heart that's true,
  Twisted virtues, a path that's new.
  A journey through malevolence, brimming with energy,
  Twisted virtues, a path of tranquility.

The Memories that Haunt

The agony of heartbreak,
A pain like no other,
It pierces through my soul,
Like a dagger, a spear, a thunderbolt.
The tears that fall,
They burn my face,
The grief that grips me,
It's a hopeless, endless race.
The memories that haunt me,
They torture my mind,
The love that once was,
It's left me behind.
The agony of heartbreak,
It breaks me apart,
It shatters my spirit,
It tears me apart.
The love that I had,
It's gone, it's dead,
The agony of heartbreak,
It fills me with dread.

Welcome to the Postmodern World

Welcome to the postmodern world,
　　Where nothing is as it seems,
　　A world of nihilism and TikTok,
　　Where reality is just a dream.
　　In this world, truth is fluid,
　　And meaning is hard to find,
　　Where memes and hashtags rule the day,
　　And the past and present blend in one mind.
　　In this world of endless scroll,
　　We find ourselves disconnected,
　　From the things that once mattered,
　　And the people that we once protected.
　　But still, we dance and lip-sync,
　　To the beat of the algorithm,
　　Hoping to find a connection,
　　In this postmodern world of spasmodic.
　　Welcome to the postmodern world,
　　Where the lines are blurred and the air is thin,
　　But perhaps in the chaos,
　　We'll find a way to let the light in.

Emotions Pouring

When emotions start pouring
    I start typing, and the words flow.
    They pour out, like a rushing river,
    They spill out, like a waterfall, that's aglow.
    When emotions start pouring
    I start typing, and the letters dance.
    They twirl and spin, on the page,
    They take on a life, of their own, and prance.
    When emotions start pouring
    I start typing, and the words take form.
    They become my outlet, and my voice
    They become my way, to weather the storm.
    So, if you see me, typing away,
    Don't judge, or criticize, or dismay.
    Just know, that I'm pouring out my heart,
    And that I'm just trying, to make sense, of the art.
    For when emotions start pouring
    I start typing, and the words just flow.
    They become my outlet, and my voice,
    They become my way, to let go, and let go.

Good Things

Good things, just got unique,
    That's the way, it is, and that's the way, it'll be.
    With a twist, that's unexpected, and surprising, and refreshing
    With a surprise, that's refreshing, and surprising, and unexpected.
    Good things, just got unique,
    That's the way, it feels, and that's the way, it looks.
    With a flair, that's stylish, and chic, and fashionable
    With a fashion, that's fashionable, and chic, and stylish.
    Good things, just got unique,
    That's the way, it sounds, and that's the way, it tastes.
    With a melody, that's catchy, and lively, and rhythmic
    With a flavor, that's rhythmic, and lively, and catchy.
So don't be afraid, to embrace uniqueness, or to celebrate
uniqueness, or to express uniqueness
    Don't be afraid, to be different, or to be special, or to be unique.
    Don't be afraid, to be yourself, or to be genuine, or to be authentic
    Don't be afraid, to be creative, or to be innovative, or to be original.
    For good things, just got unique,
    That's the way, it is, and that's the way, it'll be
    With a twist, that's unexpected, and surprising, and refreshing
    With a surprise, that's refreshing, and surprising, and unexpected.

Yeah, I've Been in Love

I've been in love.
That's what they say.
When love is blind
Ain't blind love
When love is blind and blind
Yeah, I've been in love.
Yeah, I've been in love.
Yeah, to know what to do
When I was out with my brothers
In the backseat of your cars
From the baggage and the fear
We all need to know.
Ohh, ohh, ohh
(Where would it take ya?)
To get me off our own bed
You know, it's been done before.
And you're still on the road.
Still in time, that's all right
You know, you don't need to know.
It's been done before, yeah.
You know, you don't need to know.

I am a Small God
I am a small god, in a big world,
A being of power, that's been unfurled.
I wield the elements, and command the seas,
A small god, with great abilities.
I am a small god, with a mighty heart,
A being of magic, that's been set apart.
I shape the land, and control the skies,
A small god, with great powers to devise.
I am a small god, with a great will,
A being of strength, that's been instilled.
I rule the realms, and command the gates,
A small god, with great powers to create.
So, I stand tall, and give a cheer,
To the small god, that I hold dear.
A being of magic, that's all I am,
A small god, with a mighty plan.